THE

AUTOBIOGRAPHY

OF A

PRIVATE SOLDIER,

SHOWING THE

DANGER OF RASHLY ENLISTING.

"O, man, when in thy youthful days,
How prodigal of time;
Misspending all thy precious hours,
Thy glorious summer's prime."

Sunderland:

WILLIAMS & BINNS, BRIDGE STREET,

1838.

SUNDERLAND :—

PRINTED BY GEORGE RICHMOND,

HIGH STREET.

THE AUTOBIOGRAPHY, &c.

PART I.

DEAR reader, it is proper to state that the work now put into your hands, has been composed with a view to raise funds, to procure my emancipation from a life to me the most intolerable, a life of weariness, resulting from the absence of all honourable aims and useful duties. Picture to yourself a room crowded with inmates, by no means of the best character, or of the most orderly habits. Men jesting and swearing, women gossiping; children playing, quarrelling, and crying, scampering about, threatening every minute to upset the table or the ink, and you have but a faint idea of the difficulties under which this has been written; and to complete the climax of misery, I am doomed to bear the jibes and taunts of men whom I am compelled to associate with, and whose notions of enjoying life too often consist in exhibiting the lowest buffoonery. I hope you will not criticise too severely, a work written under such circumstances.

I was born in an obscure street, in the suburbs of the city of Edinburgh. My parents, though not wealthy, lived comfortably, and earned their living by retailing, amongst other things, and by no means the most disadvantageous, the all-powerful stimulant called whisky. I was the youngest of the family that survived, and, consequently, was the favourite. Beloved by my parents, every indulgence was lavished upon me which a kind father and a loving mother could bestow. The history of the boy from petticoats to breeches, though interesting at the time will not be so now, and I would pass over it altogether, were it not tempting to show

how "the child is father to the man." When first I was honoured with inexpressibles, as a matter of course I received the customary "hansel," and never did I feel prouder, than when, for the first time, I was able to lift from my pocket the enormous sum of one penny sterling; and to demand (with all the pride which the consciousness of possession of property inspires) sweetmeats in exchange. These being obtained, home I trudged, my sister dodging me by the way for a share of the good things; but, with that selfishness too general at a later period, I believe she met with a churlish refusal. The next event was my being placed at school, the drudgery of which, as all know, painfully contrasts with the happy, "happy days of childhood;" however I got on very well.—Here I began the common rudiments of education, became a fair scholar, and was rapidly improving, when an event occurred which arrested my progress, and gave an entirely new and disastrous turn to our family affairs.

"What great events from trifling causes spring."— My sister, who at the time was receiving the addresses of a gentleman, had been invited by him to visit the theatre. She consented, not having asked leave of my parents, trusting, alas! that it would not be discovered; my father however did learn it, and nothing could exceed the anger he displayed on her return; in the fury of the moment he ordered her out of doors. She went, and my mother accompanied her; this to a man of my father's temper was intolerable, and he was too proud to recal what he had done. He immediately took to drinking, and from that hour every thing went wrong, and a short time served to effect the ruin of his circumstances, his own character, his family happiness, and worse still, to drive him into a state of hopeless insanity! Now was the time for exhibiting the nobility and beauty of woman's love. No sooner had it pleased Divine Providence to deprive my father of his reason, and plunge him into a state of helplessness, than my mother, forgetting at once the injuries she had received in being driven from her home, by one who had solemnly sworn to protect and cherish her, for no crime, but an act of maternal affection,—no sooner did this happen, than she, with a noble spirit of magnanimity, sacrificed her own outraged feelings and devoted herself to his restoration. To man this is incomprehensible and impossible.—Woman's love alone can do it! It forgives all injuries—removes all obstacles—clears the path, if lined with briars and thorns—and proportionate to the desperation of the circumstances is the energy of its manifestation. By the blessing of God on the means employed he recovered for a while, but suffered a relapse again; my mother watched and attended him in the most assiduous and kindly manner, and again he recovered, but fell into a state of deep melancholy. He frequently attempted to take his own life, and it formed the constant occupation of my mother and the rest of my family to prevent him. To me this affliction of my father was peculiarly distressing, as I was always his favourite, and I generally accompanied him in his walks. On one of these occasions he fancied that he had appointed a person to meet him on the top of a high mountain. I watched him with the most anxious feeling, and, after a long ramble succeeded in wiling him to the house of a friend, and saving him, probably, from destruction.

In the meantime, however, my schooling went on, and having become tolerably versed in geography, of which I was very fond, and able to read Latin with facility, I was, through the kindness of my uncle, removed to a more advanced school, where having completed my studies, the time came for taking the next great step in life—the choice of a profession. This is too generally done for, and not by the individual most vitally concerned. My friends determined that I should be apprenticed to a chemist and druggist, having time allowed me to attend the classes, which would fit me for my diploma, but such, alas, was never to be the case; for in a short time you will see how wretchedly I disappointed the hopes which my fond mother was building. I went to a most respectable shop, but, unluckily for me, I was not bound, and, therefore, in some manner I remained free. I soon got on with my business as well as every thing else, for I was very apt; but here I unfortunately became acquainted with a character who I think contributed, principally, to make me what I now am: this was an old soldier, a man who had served during the Burmese campaign and had seen a good deal of the hardships and pleasures attending a military life; and, while pounding the mortar, he related his hairbreadth escapes, and the shares of plunder which fell to his lot. I listened with the greatest attention, and drank in the tales of wonder with avidity: many a time have I slipt from behind the counter and stole down to the cellar to hear Old Fleming recount his marches, his carousings, and his toils in his wild career. In one of his engagements he was unfortunate enough to lose a very valuable member, and one indispensable to beauty, —his nose; the wound had healed up and made the face appear very ludicrous, for in place of a nose he had two holes in the centre of his face, which served as a substitute for it, and many a time have I laughed most heartily at the poor old chap. Old Fleming's tales raised in my breast a kind of burning enthusiasm after the same adventures, and the cholera at that time raging very severely in the city of Edinburgh, we were kept so busy that not an hour had we to spare, neither Sunday nor Saturday, for we were continually on foot, there was such a demand for cholera medicine. Harrassed in body, tired by running about, and longing for the fancied glories Old Fleming had so often detailed, I determined to throw off my yoke of servitude, and in an unhappy moment, and without thinking of the grief which it would cause my mother and relations, I enlisted and bound myself, for the paltry sum of a shilling, to serve my king and country whilst I was able to shoulder a musket. And now, my dear reader, you have accompanied me through the happiest days of my existence, through the happy days of youth, and through the still happier days of approaching manhood, continue a little longer with me, and you shall see how the hopes raised in my young bosom by Old Fleming were realised.

PART II.

To be the slave of another is degrading enough, but when a man purchases that slavery for himself, when he voluntarily pledges himself at the bidding of another to take the life of his fellow man, how doubly shameful and disgraceful does the act appear. I saw my folly when it was too late. Many a time has the remembrance of it caused the tear to steal down my cheek when walking on my lonely path. But it was done and why regret it. I endeavoured to make the best of a bad bargain and to abide by the consequences of it. Our recruiting party, in consequence of the cholera, were removed to Kinross, a country town on the opposite side of the Firth of Forth, which holds a conspicuous part in the history of the unfortunate Mary Stuart, Queen of Scots. I was glad by these means to escape from Edinburgh, and I requested a person to go and tell my mother why I did not make my appearance at dinner time as usual. We set out on our day's march, and after a long and weary walk had nearly completed it, when a carriage hove in sight, a return chaise. Our friend (foe, I mean) the Corporal being acquainted with the driver, we were not long in striking up a bargain, and into it we all jumped, another recruit, the corporal and myself. The horses were mettle to the back bone, on we flew like chaff before the wind, and we were in Kinross in a crack. The country folks all turned out on our arrival, but our reception was quite melancholy. O, poor fellows! Lord help them; they don't know what is before them, poor things," cried one. "Ay; there is a well-dressed lad, too: how I pity his poor mother," said another. "Come along, my boys," cried the corporal; let us away and have a glass. You need it after such a day's march. As we could not see the officer that night, we received a billet, and with the assistance of our friend-foe, obtained comfortable quarters. In the morning my friend, (the greatest foe I ever had upon earth) the corporal, made his appearance. "Come, my lads," said he, "we must go to the officer." Having passed his inspection, which merely consists in seeing if you are high enough, and in asking you a few questions to see if there is any detriment in your speech, nothing was left for me and my brother-recruit but to walk about during the day, or pass it over the best way we could, for we could not be sworn in till the next day. Now I had a trial to undergo which made me shake from head to foot, but not the least in resolution. A soldier I was determined to be, and a soldier I would be. No sooner had the person whom I told to tell my mother done so, than she sent for her son-in-law, the husband of the girl who was the cause of all her woes, (for she had by this time got married) and with tears in her eyes, asked him to accompany my brother to Kinross, to pay the smart, as it is called, for me : and as no time was to be lost, they set off immediately, and arrived where I was on the night following. I was immediately sent for, and went accordingly, accompanied by my friend, the corporal, who was afraid that he was going to lose his prize, and, in place of fifteen, only receive five shillings. Standing with down-cast eyes and folded arms, the following lecture was received by me with anything but good humour.—"Well," commenced my kind brother-in-law, (not in the best temper, for he had not yet eaten anything, and sixteen miles over a bleak moor must give a man his appetite) "Well, George, you have given us a fine walk. Do you know what you have done?" I answered sulkily, "I did not ask him to come after me; and more, that he had troubled himself in vain, for I was determined to accomplish what I had begun."—"Well, my poor boy, allow me to explain my motives for coming here. Your poor mother no sooner heard of your enlistment than she sent for me, and with tears in her eyes besought me to accompany your brother thus far; and, as not a moment was to be lost, we could not wait for the coach, but had to walk every step of the road. And now we have arrived in time to pay the smart; and we will pay it, if you will promise to give up all thoughts of ever acting so foolishly again. Look before you leap, my dear lad. You do not know how many hardships a soldier has to encounter, or you would not have acted so. (Alas! he told the truth.) Commit yourself in the slightest degree, and you will be tied up to the triangle, and flogged without mercy. Think of this, and come back with us to your poor mother, who wlll break her heart if you do not." I remained unmoved; inwardly determined not to follow his kind advice.

Having been assured by the corporal that he would not attest me till he had seen them on the following morning, we left. The corporal then enquired what I thought of it? "As I told them," said I; and I am determined they shall never pay 20 farthings for me. Now, I entreat you, get up a little early, and let me be attested before they come." He said he could not get a magistrate so early in the town; but would go to a small village about a mile and a half off. "Be ready, and I will be with you by day-break; and then, my lad, all will be right." The grey dawn of morn no sooner showed itself through the lattice of the closed window-shutter, than I sprung from my restless pillow, and having washed and dressed, I made the best of my way to the abode of my friend, the corporal. "Yes, my lad, all ready," was the answer I received from him, when I knocked, and asked the question; "one glass before we start, and we'll go all the brisker:" and off we went to Mrs. Beveridge's to have a morning dram. The magistrate had just arisen, and in we went, all expectation; we were called up to his dining room, and there he administered the usual oath and put the usual questions, he signed the attestation and duplicate, and as he handed the latter to me I perceived the sigh heave from his bosom, as he said "I hope, young man, you will never regret what you have done, and what you have this morning ratified." "I hope so, sir," and we made our exit. "Now my lad," said my friend, "they may whistle jukes to a milestone, you are as safe as if the devil had you." "Come let us have another drop and then we will go back and show them the attestation." Accordingly we trudged our way back to Kinross. I left it free, I returned bound: I left it without a claim, but 20 shillings would have discharged, I returned a slave, under the penalty of as many pounds. My friends had just arisen, and were coming up the street as we were going down. "Well George, my lad, will you go home with us?" "No, I can't, I was sworn in this morning to serve my king and country; so there is no use in saying any more about it. Thunderstruck at the news, my kind relatives stared, and accused my friend of a breach of promise. "It was his own fault," said the corporal, "ask him and he will tell you; he was 24 hours enlisted, and it was more than I durst do not to attest him." Having examined the attestation, and being satisfied that all was right, or rather wrong, my brother-in-law said,—"Well, George, you have done for yourself; you might have been a gentleman, but you would not; you have made yourself a mean, despicable object, and I prophecy that you will regret it every day you live. Let us go, John," to my brother, "nothing can now be done;" and the look that he gave me, the look of genuine pity, still lives in my memory as if it were but yesterday. My poor mother, when she heard of the end of their mission, exclaimed " Oh my poor beguiled child!" but no tear rolled down her cheek, her grief was too poignant to admit of such relief.

My days were now spent pleasantly enough, having nothing to do. It was a great relief to me, when compared to the close confinement which I had in my former occupation, walking about on the banks of the loveliest of lakes, viz. :—Loch Leven, inhaling the invigorating air, and playing with very idleness. My time passed very merrily; nothing to do but eat, drink, and sleep: such was my happy lot for a fortnight. But my distressed friends could not be easy on my account; they thought that they could yet rescue me from my present bonds, and applied that I might be sent for to Edinburgh, to undergo a medical inspection, as my eyes were never very strong; but they, to my present grief, were found as strong as a soldier requires. Their application was granted; I passed the medical inspection, and was reported fit to serve His Majesty. After having been proclaimed, I felt a little easier in my mind, for I was afraid of not passing, and I was ashamed to hold up my head before my old companions. All being settled, I was anxious to be off to Kinross again, as soon as possible. I prevailed on the corporal to quit a place which had now become irksome to me, and I, or rather we, quitted that loveliest of all cities, and bade adieu to home, for now every place was a home to me. Many weeks flew away before I left the lovely banks of Loch Leven. We went by way of Glasgow, where we were detained two weeks, waiting the sailing of a packet. It was in the month of November when we left the far-famed Clyde. The wind was high, and drove the clouds triumphantly before it. We stopped at a small place called Campbletown, in the West Highlands. This is a sort of half-way-house for passengers crossing the Irish Channel. Here, having laid in a stock of provisions, we started on our way. When turning an immense hill, which bounds the little bay on which the town is built, and which forms an excellent shelter to the many little fishing-boats, which run, as it were, into it for succour from the overwhelming wind, which blows at times tremendously from the Irish coast. Having weathered round the hill, we caught the wind right in the teeth. It blew a tremendous hurricane; not a tatter of sail was left unfurled; nothing was to be seen but the bare masts and the white and black chimney. Still we continned to force our way, against wind, tide, and weather. I remember sitting with my back to the funnel, watching the bleak and barren rocks, which rose on our right, for two hours; and I am fully convinced, we were further away from our destined port at the end of that time than we were at first. At length the wind had completely wreaked its fury and abated. We then made good our way, and drove across the Channel in a very short time. At this time the days were nearly at the shortest, and night was already beginning to set, before we had dropped our anchor, and trimmed our sails, to spend the first night on that dangerous element, the sea. I now, for the first time, wished myself home again with my poor mother. Again the wind freshened, and, in a short time, it blew so fiercely that it defied all our efforts to resist it. We could not weather round the immense rock under which we had taken shelter; and the captain reckoning the bay of Campbletown a safer harbour than the place where we then were, ordered the head of the vessel to be turned towards the friendly port, which offered refuge from the dreadful storm. All hands were immediately turned up to trim the sails, and to make for the place of shelter we had left. The sea ran so high that we were obliged to leave the anchor. Once more we crossed the Channel, and once more we moored alongside of that bleak, cold town. But bleak as it was, it contained some of the warmest hearts that ever I have encountered in my weary life. Of course the captain would not trust himself again on the treacherous deep, until the wind had abated, and he had a better hope of making our port good. It was of no use waiting in the abominable vessel any longer; our temporary commander, therefore, an old staff-sergeant, went and drew billets for us in the town. I, being the best dressed, as well as, I flatter myself, the best learned recruit of the three, became the sergeant's comrade. The old sergeant having been in the town before, knew where to look for the most comfortable lodging. The one which he fixed upon was a small inn, kept by a widow and two lovely daughters. The daughter second in charge of the hospitable little inn, declared I was the very picture of her beloved George; and, therefore, treated me with the kindness and affection of a sister. I fed with them; I had the best bed in the house after their own; and in their little house I was a most welcome guest. I stopped here three days, and regretted the wind would not allow us to remain longer. I left their humble but welcome roof with more regret than I did that of my poor mother, rendered miserable by my folly. However, I could not remain there for ever, and having stolen a kiss from her of whom I was fondest, I took my leave with a heavy heart.

We made a little better success this time; and having crossed once more the Channel, we saw the spot where we had lain all night four days back; and the wind not being so strong as it was before, we weathered the point, and came into full view of the Giant's Causeway, which is by far the most splendid phenomenon of nature I ever beheld. In a short time we had entered the river Foyle, on whose banks lies the far-famed city of Londonderry. The poor sick creatures, who had not been able to lift a head, or raise an arm to help themselves, began now to stir, when they were told that four hours' sail would bring them to the long wished for port. Bundles were pulled down from the recesses which they had filled, and clean clothes were pulled out of these bundles; baskets were examined, and a little was taken for the first time, of those provisions which, to all appearance, had been laid in with no sparing hand; looking-glasses were now in requisition, and combs were not idle, for, deprive a woman of her toilet, and you render her useless. I got several invitations to come down, and see my companions in the voyage; but though I promised to visit a few, and thanked them kindly for the invitation, yet I kept none of my promises; for, when I arrived at Londonderry, a new life opened before me. I had been useful to the fair sex during our emigration; for, though not in excellent health, yet I was in a much better state than any of them. I could walk up stairs for a little water when it was required; and I could hold the head of the sick, while labouring under the most dreadful affliction that I believe it possible for human beings to be troubled with.

The spire of the long looked for Derry at length appeared; and happy, very happy were the inmates of the vessel. We landed in due time, and parting with my companions, made the best of our way to the barracks.

We arrived between three and four o'clock in the afternoon. As we entered, the regiment was just forming on parade; and the hum of voices was to be heard, calling the names of the men, to see if all were present. The barracks were built in a very low part of the town, on the brink of the river; and when there was a full tide, one-half of the barrack-square was full of water. I had the good luck to be posted in a company, which inhabited the rooms farthest from the river; and, therefore, I was never under the disagreeable necessity of stepping up to the knees in water, as I rose out of bed in the morning; or finding my clothes and boots swimming about the room, which was the case with the poor fellows who resided in the lower end of the square.

After being before the adjutant of the regiment, the first thing a soldier has to do, is to introduce himself to his future companions; and the first salute which he will very probably receive, will be, " You bloody raw-headed ' Gulpin,' where do you come from?" I was shown the room in which I was to reside; and having entered it, I was asked many questions:—" Who enlisted me?" " Where I enlisted," &c. Having given satisfactory answers to the various querists, I was shown the bed which I was to occupy during the hours of darkness.

Figure to yourself a large room on the ground floor, with a couple of tables standing in the centre, nearly extending from end to end; on it, heaped in glorious confusion, lay a mass of articles appertaining to the profession of arms. Firelocks without locks, and locks without firelocks; havresacks, some half and some quite empty; pipe clay dishes, blacking boxes, blass ball boxes, and old cotton stockings, in immense heaps.— Shelves ran along the centre of the room, on which lay the knapsacks and clothing belonging to the men, all regularly piled; other necessaries, also, in neat and regular heaps are packed on them. Pegs are driven under these shelves, on which are hung the belts and accoutrements. The bedsteads are iron, neatly wrapped up; and on them in neat folds, lay the blankets, sheets, and rugs, which form the clothes of the beds. Add to these, clean-washed bricks, and a roaring fire in the grate; corners screened off for married people; a mass of men running here and there, shouting and cursing; females nursing their children, or cooking their victuals at the fire; children playing about, or crying most profusely; and you have a complete picture of a soldier's barrack room.

I slept soundly on my pallet of straw, for I had had no sleep the night previous; and I well recollect how I was awoke the next morning, by a voice by no means musical, "Come, rouse up, my lad, and see and learn to make up your bed, for you are now a soldier." I was on my feet in an instant, and the kind-hearted sergeant instructed me to fold my blankets and make my bed. I soon picked up this part of my duty; and having performed it satisfactorily, I had the gratification to be told I would be a fine soldier yet; and I believed it, for

> "The love of praise, howe'er concealed by art,
> Reigns more or less, and glows in every heart;
> The proud, to gain it, toils on toils endure;
> The modest shun it but to make it sure."

I was proud of this decided mark of a superior's approbation, and tried to deserve it the more; but though I appeared outwardly at ease, there was a strong internal struggle. The dreadful swearing filled my mind with horror, for I had been religiously brought up, and the conduct of most of the soldiers disgusted me before I had been an hour in their company. Breakfast time arrived, and down I sat to one pound and a half of bread, and a basin of coffee, which was the breakfast of the men at that time. I ate heartily, for I had not taken food during my transportation from one country to the other. I was now like a man lost. I was moving in a different sphere to that in which I had lived before. I was among a set of men entirely unknown to me, beginning an existence which I already abhorred. My very soul shrunk within me when I contemplated my future existence. I sincerely regretted that my kind relation's advice had not been taken, but it was now too late.

"Come, my lad," said a corporal to me, "you are wanted to go to the hospital to pass the doctor;" and off I went with a sergeant, for that purpose. Having undergone his inspection, which was final, I again returned to barracks; got my clothing, was enrolled in a mess, and from that hour fully entered on a soldier's life.

"Turn out for drill," resounded through the rooms at two o'clock, as the bugle sounded in the square; and out we had to run to the drill-ground. But I dare say nine tenths of my readers could not guess where that drill-ground was; it was upon the walls which surrounded the city. Tremendous walls they were, they would admit of a carriage and four driving along on them, accompanied by a troop of dragoons. Having arrived at the drill-ground, on the immense walls, we had to go through the rudiments of our drills, which was swinging a pair of heavy clubs, and making them fly round and round like the shafts of a wind-mill. Having performed this manœuvre for the space of ten or fifteen minutes, we halted, as tired as overrun horses. Having passed an hour at this play, we marched home, and passed the rest of the day in lifeless idleness. Weeks and months flew away in this sort of nonsense; and that is what is called learning the profession of arms.

There is no situation in life in which a man has a better opportunity to study man than in the army.—There you mix with all sorts of characters, from the comical to the tragical, if I may be allowed such an expression. Some are full of life, and some are as solemn as the grave; some are happy, others are dull; some are sober, (the fewest in number) others are the most detestable drunkards; some are religious, (but, like the sober, they are very scarce) and others care not for God or man. You have to associate with the most ignorant, and, in a few instances, with the brightest of men; for the army is not without its men of genius.

The most common vices among soldiers, are drunkenness, and the abominable practice of swearing. There are some who seldom, or never let a word fall from their lips but it is accompanied by the most infamous oaths. And still, such were then, and still have to be, my constant companions. It was this abominable practice that caused me to take such a dislike to military life. The first day that I entered it my mind became scared with the continued vice, until I became so much accustomed to it that I never heeded it; for if a word was said in reproof, your answer would be "what the h——l have you to do with me, you will not be answerable for my deeds or words;" and one is naturally so disgusted with the beings who defile themselves in such a manner, that any one would let them have their own way rather than run the risk of being insulted.

I was getting on rapidly with my drill, and all things were going on well, when I had to undergo the painful, very painful task of seeing a soldier flogged.— The square was formed—the triangles placed—the sentence of the court-martial read—the victim tied—and the punishment began. The poor fellow stood it very well, he only groaned under the lash.—The punishment must be dreadful. O, may God grant that I may never have to undergo such a disgrace, for I think that my heart would burst; I would prefer being shot, at least I think I would. But the crime was a bad one; and if there was not some severe punishment inflicted upon men for crime, no man could live in the army, for so many different characters and tempers exist in it, that there would be no end of vicious practices, unless there was some heavy punishment to deter men from committing them. But, nevertheless, I should be happy to see the punishment of flogging entirely abolished, and I have no doubt but (if God wills) that I will see that day when some other means may be adopted for the more effectual prevention of crime; for I have never seen a man that flogging made any better, but rather worse, for his character must sink to so low an ebb in his own eyes, that he never thinks of reclaiming it.

There is nothing that has so much interest for a soldier as a route, in fact, all soldiers are interested in a route, because all are equally concerned, every one has the march to perform, and every mind is conjecturing what like quarters are the next we are to occupy. Many are married men, and they have to look out, not only for themselves, but for their wives and children; besides, wehn the route comes for a corps to march, all is bustle and confusion: packing boxes, loading waggons, giving over barracks, and innumerable other necessary arrangements have to be made previous to the starting of the men. We are never allowed to remain long in one place. I never could understand the policy of shifting about so often; and I must obey the orders of my commander, if not without note, at least without comment. The route arrived, and the arrangements being all completed, we left the barracks of Derry. The morning was dreadfully wet, and the march was therefore very disagreeable. However, there was no remedy, on we must march; every thing on us was as wet as if we had been dipped in the Foyle. The band played an enlivening air on leaving the town; but as soon as we had cleared it, that encouragement was dropped, and we had to trudge on our weary way. I never had felt myself so miserable in my existence; and then again I thought of the words of my kind relative. "Time and tide will wait for no man," neither can 12 miles, although they are Irish ones, last for ever: inches, yards, and miles, were overcome, and we arrived at the town where we had to spend the night. I had been taught from infancy that the Irish people were all but barbarians, and I had come to the Sister Isle with that impression. You may conceive my surprise when I arrived at my quarters for the night, and found the inhabitants thereof not only kind, but graciously hospitable. "Husah Cathleen, put some turf on the fire, for the sougus are all wet, and put on a pot of potatoes for their dinner," said our host. He also showed us a room where to put our arms and accoutrements, where they would be safe till wanted; and altogether treated us as brothers. There were four of us billeted on him, which, I must allow, was rather burthensome on a poor man and with a small house. I will say this for Ireland, I have traversed it from north to south, and from east to west, and I never was harshly used or maltreated. I dare say that the cause of the hospitality shown to soldiers (who must be utter strangers) arises from this—that there are few families among the poorer classes in Ireland who have not some relative in the army—some brother, cousin, nephew, or other relative; possibly the sweatheart may be a soldier; and for the sake of those, perhaps undergoing the same toil, we receive the sympathy due to them. When morning dawned, we arose, and received orders for the day. I was appointed as one of the baggage guard, and a toilsome duty it was. On Saturday we arrived at our journey's end, that is, Donegal, which was the town we were in. I was wearied but perfectly well—something occurred in the evening which put me in low spirits during the remainder of the night.

There is only one thing of which I am fond in the army, and that is music. The music is sublime: it always raises me above myself. But that which I am fondest of, is a choice of voices accompanied by the deep swell of the organ, or the touch of the bass violin. This it is which raises a man (at least it always does me) above the limits of this transitory world. The soul, as it were departs from this tenement of clay, and pours itself out in grateful harmony to its Creator. But to my tale. The band was called to amuse the people, from whom we received great kindness of treatment. A large assembly was collected round it; but they could not hem in the sound of the instruments, although they hemmed in the performers. No; it came sweeping along in the sweetest melody. The tunes selected, at least one of them, as " Home, sweet home!" Oh, heavens, how that melancholy air thrilled through my frame! It made me shake from head to foot. I turned away, and wept; for I truly felt that there was no place like home. But then, alas! it was too late. This little incident harassed me so much that I was not myself all night: my soul departed from my body, and soared to home. I again was with my mother, sitting with my sister and brothers, happy in their smiles, and listening to their talk, and rejoicing with them; but it was only in mind; for, oh, my body was far, far away, even as far away as Donegal. My dreams partook of the same delightful theme, and I was again at home. It is amazing how quick thought can fly. It wings its flight from one corner of the earth to the other, and from earth ascends even to heaven. It is only thought, but that is consoling. The body may be shackled, but the mind defies the power of thraldom; nothing can confine it to any certain place; no, the body may be here, but the mind may be *yonder*.

Nothing occurred during the remainder of that march worthy of notice, except that it was a long one, and that I concluded it riding in a donkey's cart, for I was completely done up. The men arrived shortly after, and all hands were immediately turned out, fatigued as they were, to go and unload baggage, which is not very agreeable after a day's march; but there is no remedy, out you must turn, if you are not able to lay your legs under you (the only remedy is to put yourself in the sick report, and then you will have to go to a place not very agreeable for you, viz. the hospital, which is only for the reception of the sick. After the baggage is unloaded, and all other business done, the general place of resort is the canteen, and there is generally such a demand for refreshment, that there is not any possibility of all being waited upon, so some must wait upon themselves.

The assizes came on during the short stay of the head quarters in the town of Castlebar, at which a man was sentenced to pay the utmost rigour of the law, viz.: —he was condemned to die by the hands of the executioner. But although found guilty by a jury of his own countrymen, he still denied the fact of having murdered his wife. "I am innocent," said the condemned man. The day arrived on which he was to suffer. An immense assembly was gathered in the green, which was opposite to the jail. The moment drew nigh when the unfortunate man was to give up his life to that God who had given it to him. The priest had not been idle during the hours of the morning. "Absolve me from my other sins," said the poor man, (he was a member of the church of Rome) "but I do not require absolution for the crime for which I am this day to suffer. I am innocent." Moments flew away; at last the rope was visibly seen to move—the suspense was dreadful—every eye was intently fixed on the one spot, for every one felt an interest in the poor man's fate, who still declared he was innocent. The trap was raised on which he was to stand, and the door was slowly opened; the victim appeared, leaning on the arm of the clergyman, who was pouring into his ear the necessity of confessing the crime of which he had been found guilty, by a jury of his own countrymen; but his answer was,—"would you have me to confess a murder of which I was never guilty, and by that confession, make my last words on this earth an infamous lie. Shackled, as usual, he stood before the assembled multitude, and addressed them in the following manner:—"My countrymen, I have been found guilty of a crime the most heinous in the sight of God and man; but I declare, with my last dying breath, that I am as innocent, of the foul charge for which I am this day to die, as the child unborn; and instead of having murdered my dear wife, I loved her better than father, mother, sister, or brother." During this harangue an awful silence had prevailed, but no sooner had it been made, than a low wailing, so peculiar to the Irish, commenced among the immense crowd of spectators. He stepped out npon the fatal drop, and stood a minute in silent, but fervent prayer; he gave the signal—and was launched into eternity. But what made the scene so very peculiar remains yet to be told. No sooner had he been thrown off, than a mighty rushing noise, as if carriages were running at a furious rate, was heard coming down an adjoining street; but no carriage was there. Not a man stood of all the immense crowd; all had heard, and no one knew what he had heard. However, every one took the precaution of using his legs; but with all the rush of the great mass, nobody knew from what they were making their escape.

In finishing this chapter, I will give the two opinions which prevailed amongst the people who witnessed the execution. Some said it was angels carrying his soul to heaven, others said it was the devil dragging his soul to hell. Reader, I was one of the spectators, and I was, also one who used my legs to carry me from—I knew not what.

The assizes not only condemned one man, whom I believe to have been innocent of the crime laid to his charge; for the reason, that I do not believe there is a human being on the face of the earth, who bears the name of Christian, would plead innocence till his last moments, if he were guilty; there is something so dreadful in the very idea of being for ever shut out from the glorious presence of Almighty God, and being consigned to the tortures which hell is represented to abound with;

and it appears to me, that the most hardened wretch could not brave the horrid idea for the sake of letting the people of this world think he died innocently. I think such a thing is impossible.

They also sentenced a considerable number to transportation, for different periods. It became the painful duty for the men of our regiment to escort the convicts as far as Galway, to which place our head quarters had been shifted ; but a detachment of two companies remained. I was one of the men whose duty it was to go on escort. I travelled the same road with male prisoners first, and shortly after with females.

The time to which I am now going to refer, was the second time that I travelled that wearisome road, on that accursed duty. We marched out of the town, and made good our way at an early hour, for the march was short ; but the nezt day's march was 36 English miles, or 28 Irish ones, from Balinobe to Galway. We started long before daylight, and got into a small village, where we got breakfast, at 9 o'clock ; we had 21 Irish miles to go over yet, and the very thought of it still makes me shudder. The day set in thoroughly wet. The roads became almost impassable, with the continued rain. The prisoners were riding on a cart, but we had to keep up with them, let them drive quick or slow. That day is stamped upon my memory with an indelible mark which will never be forgotten. I was completely done up, not very far from the town where we halted for breakfast, aud I had to get upon a cart, which was used to carry the knapsacks, and to give a lift to any of those who were done up. I was among the first who became a burden to the poor old horse, which had to plod through thick and thin. I remember the place I selected was one of the worst, it was the front of the cart, and the wind and rain battered in my face without mercy. O, God, the horror of my mind on that day. I was stiff with cold and wet, and hardly able to descend from my elevated position on the cart, when we arrived at the place where we had dinner ; but a blazing fire put life in us, while we were in its vicinity : and it, also, made us colder and stiffer after we left its cherishing warmth.

Having dined, we again set off, and got to our journey's end about eight o'clock in the evening of that memorable day. We had been out sixteen hours in the most dreadful rain. On the last day we halted in a country house. Having got some dinner we were a little refreshed. A piper was sitting in the corner, and, of course, he was playing for the soldiers who honoured the house with their custom. Wearied as I was, a glass of whiskey, a few potatoes, and a piece of butter put new life into me; up I sprung, accoutred as I was, to dance a jig with Molly Ashtoe. We danced till I was ready to drop with exhaustion; all was forgot at that happy moment, and nothing but the pleasure of a dance was thought of.

Soon after this I obtained a furlough, and returned to my long lost home, for a short period. But want of space here warns me to conclude, but I cannot do it without warning young men, who are all more or less unsettled in their plans, against embracing a soldier's life.

THE END.

Printed by G. RICHMOND, Bishopwearmouth.

9 781535 811699